CRUDE A

Poems

Suzanne Cleary

BkMk Press
University of Missouri-Kansas City
www.umkc.edu/bkmk

BkMk Press
University of Missouri-Kansas City
5101 Rockhill Road
Kansas City, MO 64110
www.umkc.edu/bkmk

Executive Editor: Robert Stewart
Managing Editor: Ben Furnish
Assistant Managing Editor: Cynthia Beard

Financial assitance for this project has been provided by the Missouri Arts
Council, a state agency.

Library of Congress Cataloging-in-Publication Data

Names: Cleary, Suzanne, author.
Title: Crude angel : poems / Suzanne Cleary.
Description: Kansas City, MO : BkMk Press, University of Missouri-Kansas
    City, [2018]
Identifiers: LCCN 2018045140 | ISBN 9781943491179 (alk. paper)
Subjects: LCSH: American poetry--Women authors. | American poetry--21st
    century.
Classification: LCC PS3603.L4553 A6 2018 | DDC 811/.6--dc23
LC record available at https://lccn.loc.gov/2018045140

ISBN: 978-1-943491-17-9

This book is set in ITC Highlander, Minion Pro, and Sava Pro.

Acknowledgments

I thank the editors of the magazines and websites in which these poems, sometimes in slightly altered forms, first appeared:

5 A.M. "Famously Inhospitable"

Agenda "Apparently, There are Hundreds," "My Father's Feet"

Fifth Wednesday "Theremin"

First Inkling "Turquoise Shoes"

Georgia Review "Elm Street," "Dubbing Room"

Margie "Song After Years for the Couple Who Owned the Country Pub"

New Ohio Review "First Place," "Nest"

Nimrod "Against Nostalgia"

Poetry Daily "Elm Street"

River Styx "Making Love While Watching a Documentary on Lewis and Clark"

Sewanee Review "Edward Hopper's Paint Box," "Woodpecker"

Southern Poetry Review "Spearmint"

Southern Review "Poem for Achille Degas"

Southword "I Have Never Slept with an Animal"

Theodate "Giorgio Morandi Spent His Life"

Valley Voices "You Never Know"

Village Voice "Sausage Candle"

I am grateful for inclusion in the anthologies *Reflecting Pool: Poets and the Creative Porcess* ("Sausage Candle"), *Rabbit Ears: TV Poems* ("Lawrence Welk"), *Slant of Light: Women Writers of the Hudson Valley* ("Bird of Paradise"), and *Like Light: 25 Years of Poetry &Prose By Bright Hill Poets and Writers* ("Horse Jacket"). Jo Shapcott chose "Truthfully" for top ten finalist for the 2017 *Fish Anthology*.

Mary Noonan chose "I Have Never Slept with an Animal" as Third Place winner for the Gregory O'Donoghue International Poetry Prize of the Munster Literature Centre, Cork, Ireland. Imtiaz Dharker and Michael Symmons Roberts chose "Secret of Happiness" as Second Prize Winner of the 2017 Troubadour International Poetry Prize. "Perseids Meteor Shower" was performed as "Falling Stars," by composer Nathan Currier, at the Monadnock Music Festival.

I am grateful for residencies at the MacDowell Colony and Yaddo, where several of these poems began.

I thank Mara Bergman, Carl Dennis, Ben Furnish, Al Maginnes, and Dana Roeser: dear readers, dears. To my friends, both colleagues and students, at the Converse College low-residency MFA Program in Creative Writing: I learn from each of you.

for David

Contents

I

11 Horse Jacket

13 Elm Street

14 Bird of Paradise

16 Apparently, There Are Hundreds

18 Poem for Achille Degas

20 Love Letter

22 Perseids Meteor Shower

23 Night Sky Team

25 Snake River

26 Angel of Light

28 My Family Rides Horses Once and Never Again

29 Lawrence Welk

31 Toychestra

32 Making Love While Watching a Documentary on Lewis and Clark

II

35 I Have Never Slept with an Animal

36 Sausage Candle

37 Burt Reynolds Museum

38 Lassie

40 Art & Life

41 Thank You, Morgan Fairchild

43 Cross-Country

III

47   Election Day Robocall

48   One-Day University

50   Against Nostalgia

52   Gertrude Stein

53   You Never Know

56   My Father's Feet

58   First Place

60   Toy Harp

62   I Will Wash Your Stockings

63   Giorgio Morandi Spent His Life

64   Turquoise Shoes

65   Sally, I Need You to Stand beside Me

67   The Sun

69   Woodpecker

70   Famously Inhospitable

71   Edward Hopper's Paint Box

72   Secret of Happiness

74   Truthfully

75   Song After Years for the Couple Who Owned the Country Pub

76   20th Century Suitcase

78   Nest

81   Theremin

83   Crude Angel

85   Spearmint

87   Dubbing Room

I

Horse Jacket

I am the woman who bought the mustard-yellow
denim jacket, painted across its back the head of a turquoise

horse, its mane orange, its eyes lime green, acrylic paint
so thick the jacket was heavy as a wet newspaper. God,

I loved that jacket. From the front it looked almost
respectable: practical, made to last. From the back

it looked like a carousel from Hell. Hell, I wore that jacket
day and night, from late adolescence into late-arriving

adulthood, a jacket fit for all seasons, if any at all,
wore it home the day I bought it at the 23rd Street flea market,

from a woman who had hung each of her hand-painted jackets
on a wire hanger, lifted each hanger onto the chain-link fence.

I was 19 years old, she the age that I am now, her hair gray,
her eyes gray, her nail polish flat black. She wore a red jacket,

raised her arms and spun like a ballerina to show me,
It's ears are wrong. It doesn't look like a horse,

which was true but irrelevant, as her brief dance attested.
The mustard-yellow jacket draped a metal chair, waiting

for a woman who had left a ten dollar bill, said
she'd return with the rest of the money, disappeared.

It's yours, Honey, for the difference, the woman said,
and I bought that jacket for ten dollars and change,

for the promise it held of a life like no other. I wore it
without irony. I wore it with love. I hand-washed it

in cold water. I wore it from apartment to apartment,
those years I moved almost yearly, thinking

I would know my home as I had known my jacket:
the moment I saw it. Home would be the place where I, too,

would work on my art until late at night,
as did the woman who held her mustard-yellow jacket

for the last time, as I slipped my arms into the sleeves,
as she told me again how to care for it, as if the jacket

were a pet she was giving away, as, in fact, it was.
It was her horse, and now it was mine.

Elm Street

I am so happy to see the man who lives in the house on the corner
      sit on the porch with a guitar on his knee, one arm draped
            loosely, as if he patiently scans a vast repertoire, choosing

which song to play, or as if he has stopped midsong
      to tighten a string, then decided to listen to Elm Street
            and compose a new song, notes his fingers will find and follow,

for Elm Street is a steep hill that draws skateboarders like a magnet,
      that makes drivers roll down the truck window and stick an elbow out.
            Elm Street has been here since before it had a name, dirt path

from hilltop to river. I am happy if the man is new to the guitar, pauses
      in the middle of the only song he knows, because he has lost his place
            or lost touch with the touch he has learned to imitate, late nights

in his attic-room rental, this middle-aged man who works second-shift,
      home now for the night, which he will fill, perhaps, with song,
            or with stray notes that make song of the silence between them,

for sometimes song is beyond our reach, as found the art student
      who dutifully copied masterpieces until he saw his true gift: forgery.
            For a brief time, he built a life on copying Matisse,

for his simple line, unable to see that the line halted when the painter paused
      to look at his model. The line resumed with hesitance, a quaver
            the forger never could replicate, conceding,

I mastered his line, it was his pause I could not master—finally having seen
      that to see the model is to quaver in her presence, is to carry forward
            what little you can balance on the tip of the brush.

Silence, big silence that surrounds us, some of us dare to hear you.
      Tonight, I am happy it is the man on the corner, instead of me,
            who sits in your presence, and readies himself to play.

Bird of Paradise

Bird of Paradise quilt top,
1858-1863, vicinity of Albany, New York

In Albany, New York, circa 1860, no one had seen
the tropical flower named Bird of Paradise,
that orange and violet pinwheel of petals,

the Bird of Paradise quilt depicting birds
of upstate New York, imperfect paradise
of crow, grackle, turkey, a patchwork

quilt of wool and cotton scraps, their dark colors
drawn from bark and nut, from the brief flowers
of a cold place. Do you imagine a farm woman

could work on this quilt for five years
and not be thought a fool,
not ask herself, some nights, *Why?*

Do you imagine that she did not dream of the day
she could be done with it, pull the quilt
over her head, and sleep,

even as she delighted over three linen eggs,
laying them perfectly atop a muslin nest?
Despite the quilt's depiction of actual birds,

do you think that this woman did not understand
bird of paradise as metaphor,
she who lived not far from towns named

Rome, Ithaca, Carthage, Painted Post?
You work with what you are given.
Any farm woman knows this,

knows that paradise, like a bird,
lights on earth for brief moments.
Here, paradise spreads its wings

as a girl's long hair lifts upon the breeze,
or as a blanket floats briefly over,
then upon, summer grass,

bluebells soon to be covered in snow.
If someone brought to this woman's dark parlor
the tropical flower Bird of Paradise, and set it in water,

what do you think she would do?
Do you not think she would sit, and work
by the orange and violet flame of that flower,

its light so like that of a candle,
so like what burned inside of her
as she slid her needle through, back through,

the fabric? For that matter,
weren't they one and the same to her—
a flower, a bird—and both of them

amenable to what she would make of them
in the paradise of her work,
from which she would not fly?

Apparently, There Are Hundreds

Apparently, there are hundreds of pianists
      who play the piano while upside-down, lying back
across the bench, their heads below the keyboard,

eyes staring at the underside of the instrument.
      They bend their arms as if carrying a stack of wood,
so their hands can dangle above the keys,

Flight of the Bumblebee, Dueling Banjoes,
      Rhapsody in Blue, any song with lots of notes
crushed together, the pianists' fingers rushing

like time itself. Fast they play, too fast,
      no less the frail woman in a violet housecoat
than the crew-cut man in gym shorts,

no less the ruddy woman freckled as a trout,
      whom you think you have seen somewhere, maybe
yesterday, ahead of you in line at the grocery store,

counting coupons slowly into the cashier's palm.
      You had no idea she had such talent. And
maybe her child, too, pulling Chiclets from the wire rack.

And how many others in the Grand Union?
      Should you try this stunt yourself? One
YouTube pianist prefaces his performance,

I know this hymn so well I can play it upside-down,
      suggesting, one day, a miracle: as he sat to play
his body spun, his head dipped back

like a river baptism, and *Praise God*
      from Whom All Blessings Flow
flowed, a torrent, from his fingertips.

Like you, he'd had no idea such a thing
        was possible. Like you, he'd thought
he was alone, despite his professions of faith,

 alone, until God revealed Himself to him
        in this talent for playing upside-down
the simple hymn, a rendition with more notes

than strictly necessary, with too many notes,
        some would say, too theatrical, like these
versions of *The Maple Leaf Rag, The Minute Waltz,*

not to mention the songs from the transistor radio
        of your childhood: *Goldfinger, A Taste of Honey,*
The Girl from Ipanema, the girl who is now 75 years old,

whom you saw once, on TV, wearing long turquoise earrings,
        saying she'd inspired the song simply walking
on the beach, touching, now, one finger to her wild white hair.

Poem for Achille Degas

after *Scene from the Steeplechase: The Fallen Jockey*, by Edgar Degas

Let your brother be praised for his *fierce, expressive, abrupt strokes*,
for his daring to paint a modern-day scene, but you were the one

who lay twisted on your back in the wet grass of morning
while your brother sat on his little folding chair

and stared, pressing the wrong end of the pencil to his lower lip,
hours, days, weeks, the only painting done by clouds sweeping

purple scarves across the wide field, draping painter and model
alike. Monumental, this painting required numerous preparatory

sketches, in early light, sharpest shadow. The two of you rose
in the dark, in your knapsack a loaf of bread to share as you walked.

Younger brother, poor jockey but good sport, under Edgar's direction
you turned your smooth face to the light. You closed your eyes.

You lay with your hands palms-up, like two cups of blue tea
in the blue-green grass, the soles of your boots purple as twilight.

Achille, let your brother be praised for spending thirty years in that field,
working it with good nature, telling a friend, *It is one of those works*

which are sold after a man's death & artists buy them not caring
whether they are finished or not.

Let your brother be praised for his doomed commitment
to finding the ideal inside of the real, but you posed

in shiny black boots so tight that you could not walk,
your feet the real inside of the ideal. Midmorning,

shadows faint with light, you sat up, rumpled, squinting.
You worked one black boot off, then the other.

Let your brother be praised for his numinous black mixed
from greens and dark reds. You were the one

who, like a magician, put into the sack shiny black boots
but pulled out from the sack scuffed brown boots

in which you limped home to bake bread for tomorrow.

Love Letter

It's the season again
  when he wrote me a letter
    from his new house, describing

the view from the kitchen window
  where he stood washing dishes,
    turning his cup and plate and pot

under the running water
  as he looked out onto a field
    where two horses stood,

two brown horses, but one
  more golden-brown, and smaller.
    Their eyes were black and shiny

as the mud beneath their hooves,
  for it had rained most of the day,
    until dinner. He had rice

with steamed carrots and peppers,
  an apple, then a cigarette,
    trying to quit, but still

drawn to the slow pull of it, to smoke
  the blue of distance, but close.
    His neighbor's field was bound

by wire fencing bought on big wooden spools.
  An empty spool rested on its side,
    as a table, by the back door.

He had not yet met the neighbors,
  but this morning he had seen a thin
    red-haired girl with a bridle

pat the small horse on its head
        and on its rump, then turn back
                to the house. The small horse

had a black mane, the other horse
        a mane of light gray, like
                the moment day becomes *dusk,*

as if it were no longer the same day.
        He washed the dishes,
                washed the sink,

dried the counter with a towel
        as the horses watched him
                from the near corner of the fence,

which seemed their favorite place,
        where they stood close
                to each other, encircled

by hoof prints that shone
        from the mud
                like half moons,

as each letter of his daily, handwritten letter
        shone with the tenderness
                he had wanted to show me

but could not show me,
        nor I could show him,
                except in letters

where we described things we could see
        as practice for loving
                first the world, then ourselves.

Perseids Meteor Shower

MacDowell Colony, August 2008

It falls through me still,
that falling star,
as it fell through the sky,

through the other stars
that stayed fixed, it seemed,
to their spots above Mount
Monadnock,

while that one star slips
like a needle through black velvet,
one stitch, so bright, so brief

I thought I had imagined it,
until the second star fell,
and a third, and I knew

I had seen my first falling star,
which falls through me still,
as if nothing ends, not the light

and not the darkness close upon it,
not light nor memory of light,
nor the vast, replenished dark.

Night Sky Team

Zion National Park, Utah

The Night Sky Team is not Orion and Cassiopeia,
      not the Seven Sisters linked arm in arm in arm, etcetera.
           The Night Sky Team is two women and two men

who meet on the porch of the park lodge
      in hiking boots, khaki shorts with matching two-pocket shirts,
           and stiff-crowned hats. Each member of the team

carries a pocket-knife with eight features: spork, flashlight,
      knife, file, awl, mirror, toothpick, plus
           a secret compartment the size of the cap of an acorn.

At dusk, as Orion and Cassiopeia slowly appear,
      each member of the Night Sky Team appears,
           on the wooden steps before the rocking chairs,

to lead groups of tourists across the lawn, beyond
      the wide canopy of the cottonwood, beyond
           the street lamps of the parking lot, to a place

impossible to know in advance, a place suitably
      dark, to stand there, and look up.
           The Night Sky Team has a motto, *Save the Starlight.*

The night sky is part of the park, says the team,
      no less than the Navajo sandstone and the pinyon pine,
           the blue-tailed lizard. Starlight is disappearing.

Each member asks her or his group, *How much light
      do we need here on Earth? How little light
           is enough to see?*

Tonight we barely can see the belt of Orion, maybe
      his belt's dull buckle, yes, shining like a dime-sized locket
           bearing a fold-out camp chair with arms and headrest,

in which we could sit all night under the sky, staring up
at what we can see, and at what we cannot see
for the distraction of light here below,

where the Night Sky Team meets each day at dusk,
each carrying an acorn-cap ration of darkness
in the secret, waterproof compartment.

Snake River

Before I will step into the raft
        I must know why this is named
the Snake River, and I am told
        that I stand where pioneers
stood, whether they called standing here
        good luck or bad, this spot
beside a rocky-bed creek
        that floods this shore
when the rain comes.
        So I understand
it has always been thus, and wise:
        to pause, to gauge the need
for crossing here or elsewhere,
        or for crossing tomorrow
instead of today, or for crossing never.
        The guide tells me a wagon train
wound its way between mountains,
        slinking through gullies, swerving
around rocks, and stopped where I stand,
        where an Indian boy stood,
tossing stones into the water.
        The wagon master and another man
climbed down, told the boy their names,
        asked for his. The boy
gave them the name of his tribe
        by weaving his finger through the air.
We are weavers is what he said,
        but the white folk thought *snake*
in their fear, and carried their fear
        across the river.

Angel of Light

Each time you drive past the close-out store on Route 7

        you see the six-foot-tall angel shining in the front window,

gold-coated wings high above the loveseats and La-Z-Boys

        and (why so many?) end tables, things once chosen

but left unclaimed on a loading dock or, worse, delivered

        and refused, which leads you to wonder who would refuse

an angel, especially one with a three-foot wingspan, solid plaster,

        coated with something that guarantees *protection*

from the elements. Since when does an angel require protection?

        Maybe this angel requested protection because, like you,

it tends to worry, which you like to think is a sign of intelligence,

        imagination. This angel has considered the dangers

of life on earth, and still it commits. It will not quit,

        come snow, come hail, come bird, bird droppings,

come long afternoons of high summer, when even you believe

        that your life will never end. It will stand firm, the $600

Angel of Light, whose price and name you know because, once,

        you stopped. You drew your finger through the dust on its brow:

angel dusty, angel heavy, angel fated to stand in the window

        until carted to the warehouse basement, angel fated

to serve as coat rack for the young men on the loading dock, who roll up their shirtsleeves even in winter.

Each time you drive past, lifted and swept into the rush hour traffic,

you wonder, you cannot help but wonder,

if the Angel of Light, maybe the Angel of Light shows you

that the main thing is to stand still, so as better to show

the movement of light across us.

My Family Rides Horses Once and Never Again

My family rides horses once and never again, in the early 1970s,
the Sunday afternoon my father drives the green Bonneville station wagon
to a farm beyond the edge of town, and even my mother mounts, her horse
a gray named Blue, whose first and fastest move is dipping his head, yanking

a thick hank of grass, chewing, as we all laugh nervously, for we are afraid
of horses, but I, fifteen, the eldest of four, have been lobbying to ride.
I like *Bonanza*. I hope for a pair of Frye boots, which my parents say
I can buy when I get a job. I cannot believe that today, beside a corral,

we sit on six horses who kick dust, as a girl, maybe 17, small
for her age, shows us how to hold the reins. My father's horse is brown,
named Charlie Brown, and follows the girl's golden horse onto the trail,
which is a rocky path through a field unsuited to crops. My sisters and brother

and I follow, with Mom at the end. Our horses step slowly over grasses
and small stones. They flick their tails in the secret horse language
for *These flies are killing me*, or *Looky yonder at them thar thunderheads
a-fixin' to storm*, but the sky is blue, the only sound the squeak of leather

as we shift in our saddles. We are sweaty with heat, some lingering anxiety.
We hold the reins loosely, as we have been shown, ready to pull back
if need be. There is no need. The horses carry us slowly through the air,
the sound of crickets like marbles being shaken in a wooden box.

There are things done once and never again, and never spoken of again—
not for shame, nor sorrow, nor for anything a person can understand
except that some days are nothing that is not life itself, words
need not touch them. Other days, nothing exists until commented upon,

tamed into story, like a horse that has circled a wide field
to stand where it began, nosing the grasses, reins wrapped lightly
around the rail. Tell me, how does one live a life
built upon days that are mostly lost, and rarely remembered?

How does one speak of the lost, of my parents standing with all of us
in the high sun, at the edge of a field let go to gold seed? I cannot
believe we have crossed this field, twice, on six horses: through,
then back through, and for the rest of my days.

Lawrence Welk

If you were 12 years old and you wanted an accordion
and your father bought one for you, on the condition
that you'd work on the farm until you were 21, no pay
except food and a bed, then you'd be, among other things

Lawrence Welk, who had walked to town, Strasburg,
North Dakota, to the window of General Store and Pawn,
where he heard his life call out to him, from something a cross
between an encyclopedia and an upholstered wagon-spring,

an instrument hard to love unless one already loves it
and has never heard it played. Then, eventually,
you'd be the man who traveled hundreds of miles
hoisting the wide strap over your head and right shoulder

and fitting your thick hands under the patent leather straps,
pushing and pulling and pushing and pulling music
from this contraption, each song a hard-earned song,
the years on the farm paying off in muscle and stamina,

scant drops of sweat on your brow, shining like
the bubbles of champagne that would become your trademark,
your orchestra's music called *champagne music*
for the way it sparkled and rose, floating away like nothing

you'd seen on the farm except dust, and money, and years.
You'd excel in business, your Saturday night TV show
watched by millions of American grandparents, tapping toes
to Elvis Presley's "Don't Be Cruel" as sung by violinist Bob Lido

wearing Press-On black sideburns. People could be cruel,
you'd know this, but you'd never get discouraged.
You'd never ask why it could not have been a flute or a fiddle
that had called out to you, something less furniture-ish

riding your heart like the hardest moving-day ever, a La-Z-Boy
sleeper sectional-sofa wrestled up a winding staircase.
If you'd had a father who drove a bargain hard as he drove horses,
if you'd seen your father climb down from the wagon

to water those horses, to unhitch them before the heat of day,
and then stand knee deep in a dustbowling field,
could you have taken it? Yes. You would have taken from him
the $400 accordion, played it after each night's last chore, years

before you'd wear a white shirt, let alone a powder-blue suit,
let alone your hair pomaded to the shine of sweat
on the young boy you were, when you told your father
what you wanted.

Toychestra

We got together and brought our regular instruments, and I
brought some toys too. We tried both, and the toys definitely won.
—Lexa Walsh, on the inception of Toychestra

Sometimes all you need is a plastic guitar and three of your best friends

to join you on stage. But add tin piano, and balsa-wood harp, and *Scotty*,

a felt bagpipe with red balloon bladder. Add three metal folding chairs

for your friends to drag into a circle, for this song will take time,

will take time and change time into notes that sound like these chairs

scraping the wood floor, their metal feet sliding, catching,

squealing, until they circle you, and you look at your friends

and nod *Now.* Sometimes all you need is play instruments.

All you need is to toy with play, itself some measure of song,

and you as well some measure, unlikely and new.

Making Love While Watching a Documentary on Lewis and Clark

Tired from sightseeing, after our showers we got into bed,
turned on the TV, and lay hip-to-hip, watching
William Clark climb the last feet up the Continental Divide,

the spine of the Rockies, after which rivers flow west,
the camera lingering on yellow, star-shaped flowers
bobbing among tall brown grasses, as if to suggest

idealism, somehow, still pulsing in the explorer's breast,
even after hundreds of miles. We stared at the contrasts
of rocky trail and bright sky, and counted ourselves lucky

to be here, in the Best Western, far from home, true,
but without need for compass or canteen, and
with everything that Clark might have seen, unspooling

at our feet. When Clark reached the summit,
the photographer stood still, let the river say it all.
We watched that moment, transfixed, although we'd already begun

to drift, whether into sleep or into each other, we could not yet say.
The summit, we learned, was a supreme disappointment
for Clark. He had expected the Pacific, not more mountains,

snowcapped, as far as he could see, as far as he dared
imagine. Although we were starting, again, to wander—
our attention, our limbs—it seemed to us the program

had a theme: the imagined giving way to the actual.
While the others set up camp, Clark had scouted ahead,
toward what he imagined. Now, speculated the historians,

as Clark stood at the summit, he imagined his party
pitching tents, striking the night's fire. He imagined himself
returning to camp, to pronounce the journey far from over,

over another close-up shot of the yellow flowers, another
shot of the Missouri, gaining power and depth, flower, river,
flower, river, river, river, river, the actual river.

II

I Have Never Slept with an Animal

I have never slept with an animal, so it is
        a dream from which I wake: the small bulldog
jumping on the bed, scrumbling the sheets,
        stepping onto my face. His forepaws knead
my cheeks. His tongue dangles at my nose.
        He noses my hair. He pauses, stares.
He pants, his meaty heart close to mine, this
        short-legged, flat-faced dog
that sleep has conjured to wake me, wake me
        so I have no choice but to breathe
the doggy breath, to meet the rheumy eyes,
        brown-flecked-with-gold like the doors
on a Hepplewhite cabinet built to feature
        the wood's grain, sprays of rings recording
years of much rain, years of little rain,
        except that this dog, emissary from the deep,
will not be still, will hide nothing from sight.
        It is warm, pulsing, demanding, demands
that I wake, I wake now, yes, now, in a new way.

Sausage Candle

*[A]longtime Manhattan resident . . . Ms. [Fran] Lee advised radio
and television audiences on household and consumer issues from the late 1940s
until well into the '90s. Her purview ranged from cyclamates to asbestos
to how to make a candle from a sausage.*
—New York Times obituary, February 19, 2010

S

t

i

c

k

a wick in a sausage
and light it, and you've got
a candle, its flame fed by fat,
not that you'd burn it
on your birthday cake,
not that you'd light two
and process to an altar,
not that you'd want one,
even a small one, flickering
over your romantic dinner.
But the sausage candle gives light.
The sausage candle gives light.
Think of the books you could read
by the light of that candle,
think of the dark passages it might,
given the chance, illuminate.
It is better to light one sausage
than to curse the darkness.
Imagine, for a moment, you dare
set a sausage candle
atop your cake, and
you close your eyes and you wish.
Think of the wishes you could make
if you weren't afraid of the ridiculous.

Burt Reynolds Museum

I admit that I never have visited the Burt Reynolds Museum,
      but I would argue that a poem should take anyone, poet or reader,
to a place they never have been, and so I claim this museum for my own,
      although I saw it only from the car as I drove past Jupiter,
painted on a billboard on I-95: a low orange building
      behind the face of Burt Reynolds circa *Smokey and the Bandit.*
Why not? I thought as I drove. Why should money from bad movies
      not buy good art? Why should Burt not collect Cindy Sherman
or Kara Walker, early, before others caught on? I suspected
      I would never forget this promise of a long afternoon
free from the midday sun, chilling before paintings by Cézanne
      and Paula Modersohn-Becker, charcoal studies by Giorgio Morandi.
I suspected I would never forget this moment of passing the exit, lifting
      my foot slightly before speeding past my conviction
I should be walking slowly through dark galleries,
      each painting afloat in its own cone of light.
Later I read on a fan site that the museum is named *The Burt Reynolds*
      and Friends Museum, which suggests that Burt and his friends
installed each tubular bulb, flicked a little switch, then stood together
      admiring their work. I read that the museum features
not paintings, but items from Burt's life and career, including
      photographs of Burt with actors and athletes and presidents.
It is a former bank. Burt *installed smoked glass front doors, to make it seem*
      less of a bank, and to give a sense of drama to the entry—just
as in a poem, I thought, where I have installed my share of smoky glass
      doors, for lack of knowing what else to do. On the fan site I learn
[t]he canoe from Deliverance *is balanced on its nose in one corner.*
      Where, where was I driving that day? All I know is that
I had miles to go before I slept, miles beyond
      that low orange building with its darkly sparkling entry.

Lassie

for Tom

Because my brother, age three, saw a Columbus Day parade
where a horse's back opened like a drawbridge,
then one man lifted the horse head from his shoulders

while a second man, stooped, straightened up,
adjusting suspenders that had held up the horse's rump,
and then the crowd, apparently not terrified by the sight

of a horse breaking into two half-men, began cheering,
my brother, from ages three to five, believed that TV's
Lassie was two short actors inside a dog costume,

Lassie who each Sunday evening, as the closing credits
scrolled, crested a ridge and sat and lifted her paw
to the television audience, after 30 minutes

of danger and rescue, Lassie barely panting
as she held high her inexplicably convincing head.
How the actors produced Lassie's bark

remained a mystery to Tom, but he turned
his attention to the larger picture, precociously
aware that each episode told two stories:

1) the story of the athleticism of two actors,
undersized yet determined, who ran and jumped in sync
in the moist darkness of a dog costume; and,

2) the story of Timmy, an only-child
who lived on a farm with his parents and
a checkered tablecloth, a tin coffee pot, and a telephone

that hung on the wall and had to be cranked and yelled into.
For my brother, lone boy among sisters, I'm guessing
The Lassie Show was mainly the story of Timmy,

whose best friend was a dog costume. Timmy's other friends
were the two short actors. My brother learned early
that what people say about the acting profession is true:

you have to love it, because it never will be easy.
Every Sunday evening we watched *The Lassie Show*,
Tom never once saying that he thought the dog two men,

because why state the obvious? Why question what you know
to be true? Hadn't a dog circled the earth in a spaceship?
Wouldn't it live up there forever, head over heels through the stars?

Art & Life

Who among us has not pushed a block of ice through the streets of Mexico City?

Who among us has not sat cross-legged on the floor while strangers snip away our clothes?

Who among us has not smeared our body with chocolate?

Who among us has not, for 27 years, painted the same glass of water, on the same windowsill, every morning from 8 A.M. to 9 A.M.?

Who among us has not splayed our dominant hand, used a series of 20 knives to stab at the spaces between the fingers, taking a fresh knife for every stab that draws blood

and has not expounded upon this as comment upon mistakes of the past and mistakes of the present?

Who among us has not willingly enclosed ourselves in a gallery with a wild coyote?

Who among us has not extracted from a bodily orifice a long coil of paper upon which is written our response to a critic's harsh and stupid review?

Who among us has not, more conventionally, hoisted a urinal onto a pedestal?

Who among us has not shot ourselves in front of a crowd?

[Artists, in order: Francis Alys, Yoko Ono, Karen Finley, Peter Dreher, Marina Abramovic, Joseph Beuys, Carolee Schneemann, Marcel Duchamps, Chris Burden]

Thank You, Morgan Fairchild

Thank you, Morgan Fairchild,
for your demonstration of how to drink
without ruining one's lipstick.

Thank you for holding the glass of water
un-self-consciously before your full bosom,
for staring directly into the TV camera as you

rounded your *Fuchsia Dream* lips into a fish-mouth.
Thank you for saying what you were about to do
before you did it, so we knew what to look for, for

example, the pressing of the tongue against the glass,
thereby creating a seal to shield the lower lip,
for example, tilting slowly the glass while keeping

the top lip curled up, above the water. Thank you,
Morgan Fairchild, for not winking at the camera
so as to distance yourself from those of us watching,

our mouths slightly open, our heads tilting back.
Thank you for not distancing yourself from yourself,
an ageing woman who, like any of us, thirsts

to be of use, who knows from long experience
that diligence in small things can make the world
more beautiful. And thank you for not saying this.

You shone with concentration as if inside
a cone of light. You shone with a generosity
that made us want to call you *Morgan.*

You showed us not one swallow, nor two, but four
swallows, the water never once wetting your lips,
but not so as to brag. You knew that it

wasn't about you, Morgan. It was bigger than you,
that full minute when the only sound
was someone's cough and a cellophane wrapper

as you, in your high heels and high hair,
drank water in the harsh studio light,
thirty years after you were young. We saw

that, whether for an audience of 50 or 50,000,
you would always give your all.
Morgan, you are such a pro.

Thank you for raising your empty glass in toast,
swiveling at your waist like the queen of England
waving from her coach, which is more dangerous

than generally acknowledged. Thank you
for making yourself a target, a model for each of us
embarrassed to admit that we even watched you.

Morgan, you did not cure cancer.
You did not save the elephant. You saved lipstick.
Time held still. We drank it in.

Cross-Country

I.
Buster Keaton has a drinking problem,
so on the cross-country train
the film crew teaches him to play poker.

Buster Keaton has a gambling problem.

II.
Buster Keaton has a gambling problem,
so the film crew hides the deck of cards.

Between here and the next station
there will be three white horses.

Double or nothing.

III

Election Day Robocall

November 8, 2016

I had no idea that political robocalls are legal on Election Day,
     and maybe they aren't, but here I am, standing in my kitchen
          with candidate Alison Avery's recorded voice in my ear,

my mouth half-open as if I believe that Alison will pause and let me speak
     after the rush of her words, which are friendly and optimistic
          but, alas, too late, for I have just returned from voting

at the high school down the block, for I voted early this morning,
     expecting a line that extended from the gymnasium door
          to the sidewalk, extended the length of the soccer field

at the brown brick building where students are living what they will remember
     as the worst days or the best days of their lives—and which case is
          worse?—students who go home to parents born in Ecuador

or Little India, who accompany their parents to the emergency room,
     to the post office, where they stand in the long line for money orders
          to send money to the place they call home, where they stand

in the longer line to mail packages to this place. Their boxes are wrapped
     in brown grocery bags cut open and pressed flat, fastened with tape
          that the postal clerk tapes over, presses flat with what seems

excessive force as the child translates *Hazardous? Liquid? Perishable?*
     While I cast my vote I heard no voices from the classrooms' thick silence,
          although class was in session. Soon the first wave of students

would hit the cafeteria for lunch: lunch at 10 A.M., so there is time
     for everyone to eat. Alison, yes, I know that you want to serve *our county,*
          that you want to lower our taxes and clean our river, surely as I know

that you want my vote, which I cast early this morning, while the sun
     was mostly long shadows that grew steadily shorter, then paler,
          then nearly gone by the time I reached my front door,

through which I could hear my phone ringing, and it rang as I ran across
     my shiny wood floors, to hear you—your first words,
          in all the world, the words I most want to hear: *There's still time.*

One-Day University

My neighbor whose parents divorced in 1962 drives a 1961 Pontiac,
a sky-blue Bonneville Classic, with a shiny ash tray in each armrest,
with windows you have to crank down, and up again,

a car surprisingly fast despite or due to its weight, each part of steel,
not plastic or composite, whatever that is. *The gas mileage is killing me*,
my neighbor shrugs, smiling, shaking his head the way you do

when you know that something is beyond your control and the best
you can do is enjoy the ride, *killing me*. But each Saturday he wakes
early, to hose down and soap up that car, to chamois it into shine,

then he drives to One-Day University, this weekend's lecture
Lincoln and Kennedy: Imagining Their Second Terms,
a professor from Princeton University leading the assembled,

I imagine, to imagine a world in which Lincoln will trade
his stovepipe hat for a houndstooth-check driving cap,
roll his trousers, and take up golf, years into a long retirement,

to imagine a world in which Kennedy will fall in slow motion
on a wide green lawn, as he fake-tackles grandkids.
I imagine that the good professor, paid well for his time,

calls on a stand-in for each president, who thanks the assembled,
then describes his second term, the politics that never change.
Probably Lincoln would go first, with a plainspoken vision

of the world that might have been, while Kennedy sits behind him
on stage, his bad back aching from the metal folding chair.
I can imagine nothing sadder than Lincoln and Kennedy

present in the same moment,
with their strained marriages and strong children, forget
the futures we know lie immutably before them—

not to minimize the sadness of a lecture hall full of people
who have given up their Saturday to cast themselves into another day,
back, to a moment of tragedy, to imagine they can erase tragedy:

no *Our American Friend*, no convertible,
no pink pillbox hat pinned so tightly on that it never flies off.
My neighbor drives to work in 1961 and drives home in 1961.

He drives to the dry cleaner, and to the grocery, and to the gym,
to the post office, to the gym again, all in 1961,
the car window rolled down, his elbow hanging out.

Wherever he drives, he drives through 1961 to get there, imagining,
as an educated man, not a world before or without sorrow, but
a world of alternate, composite sorrows, the wind in his hair.

Against Nostalgia

Because I suspect that it is nostalgia, and I suspect that nostalgia
    is love of the self masquerading as love of the world,
        I have tried not to speak of the Woolworth's five-and-dime

at the corner of Court Street and Water. I have tried not to show
    that I remember, enjoy remembering, running my hand
        along the scalloped edge of the bolts of fabric, while the smell

of hot popcorn, at first sickening, grew distant, then delicious.
    I have tried not to admit that I savor the buttery air of Woolworth's
        as others savor the salt and brine of a youthful trip to Calais,

my Calais, circa 1965, Binghamton, New York, where almost
    anyone who had been to France had been there as a soldier.
        Veterans of World War I, The Great War, we still called it that, sat

at the Formica lunch counter, drinking coffee, cigarette balanced on the edge
    of the saucer as wide dull-bladed fans spun overhead.
        Because I suspect that nostalgia is love of love itself, unencumbered

by effort or consequence, uncomplicated by responsibility or fear,
    I have tried not to wander those aisles, where no one thing is more important
        than another: not the white anklet nor the hairnet,

not the doily nor the handsaw, nor the display where the bicycle
    and the sled stood side by side, as if there were no seasons, or all
        seasons were one. I have denied my love for the parakeets

that sang in their cages, except for the day when someone unlatched the little doors
    and the birds, like turquoise and tangerine cellophane, flew under the fans,
        over the two glass vats of lemonade, pink and pale green, ceaselessly

tumbling through themselves. Employees with butterfly nets ran that day
    through Woolworth's, where I first learned that one thing
        can be exchanged for another: a quarter for a card of shirt buttons

or a box of eight crayons, a dollar for a metal picture frame, for a rain bonnet
    that, in theory, would fit back into its hinge-topped plastic capsule,
        which I loved, that small compartment impervious to rain.

Because I suspect that nostalgia may be love of the best self, that small part
    that gives and forgives, that nostalgia at best may be practice
        for loving the present, I indulge myself in remembering

the lunch counter's red vinyl stools, reserved for the veterans, who sat
    shoulder to shoulder, talking about sports and the weather,
        who sometimes just nodded and reached

into a shirt-pocket for a pack of Lucky Strikes, tapped one out,
    offered, lit it with a flick of the wrist. I remember the economy
        of the gesture, the brief flame, the ribbon of smoke,

although I suspect that I do not remember, rather, imagine,
    as I imagine that one man carried a bullet beneath a rib,
        and another man carried a rabbit's foot spotted with blood.

Because I suspect that nostalgia may be the desire to exchange one's life
    for another life, or to exchange one version of one's life
        for another version, in which one lived more deeply,

I come down hard against nostalgia, somewhat as my chest slammed
    onto the Flexible Flier which, in truth, I never enjoyed
        except for the part where I was indoors, and warm again.

Gertrude Stein

Hollywood movies of the 1930s always show the scene
>   where a woman lifts her small suitcase onto the bed,
>   tosses handfuls of silks and satins,

flashing and shimmering as they tumble, they pool: *starlet*,
>   unlike Gertrude Stein, who travels with a leather trunk
>   big as a block of ice pulled with tongs from the river,

then hoisted with a strap onto the back, carried through woods.
>   Stein's clothes do not shine. They absorb light.
>   They are wool and linen, rough-wove cotton.

They are too heavy to throw, even if she wanted
>   to throw them, she who works slowly, deliberately,
>   large hands fitting one shoulder of the black jacket

into the other shoulder, aligning the side seams, folding
>   the jacket over her arm, laying it in, just so.
>   Stein smoothes the brown corduroy skirt,

waistband to deep hem. She traces the weave
>   of the maroon brocade vest always pinned at her waist,
>   always strained open at her unrestrained bust. No,

no resemblance between Gertrude Stein and the bottle-blond
>   who tosses her pink tap-pants into the air, following
>   the script, earning, for a time, a living,

while Stein, in Paris, in 1938, slips clothes from their hangers,
>   holds them high, high above the street soon to be packed
>   with people carrying suitcases, or sacks, or nothing at all.

You Never Know

Because you never know,
        because it's good to be reminded
that you never know, this is why

I go to junk shops, this Saturday,
        for instance, a three-foot tall bust
of Albert Einstein, from who-knows-

where, from a local Einstein
        Museum, from Einstein's House
of Pancakes, the bust a chunk of plaster

the size of a moped and formerly parked
        in a school library, or in the storeroom
of some family-run shoe store,

the family's youngest surviving child
        74 years old, *years young*,
he says, but ready to retire, move

to some place where winter
        is not a thick brow of snow
on each sill. Albert Einstein stares,

stolid atop a great-grandfather's
        roll-top desk jammed open,
drawers full of wooden shoe buttons,

until, two weeks ago, Einstein rises,
        inside of a blanket, as if he were a dog
that must be tricked into the car.

Einstein rides to the junk shop
        where he perches on a blond
coffee table, mid-20th Century, Scandinavian,

in the shadow of a brass floor lamp
        with a green shade.
Einstein looks a little green, along

the long, steeply sloped forehead
        that makes me believe
the story that Einstein failed math,

even though I recognize that the story
        endures not because it is true,
but because it is fun. It is fun to think

of a genius having failed, which makes
        of him a brother, life-size
even if four-times life-size, this bust

a monument not just to Einstein,
        but also to the sculptor, who
did not engrave his own name on the base,

and also a monument to the care
        of its nameless custodians,
those many years. I stand close.

There is no choice but to stand close
        in a crowded junk shop.
My coat sleeve touches Einstein's hair

and, you never know, I remember
        being carried on my father's shoulders,
remember Karl Walenda on the high-wire

with his daughter on his shoulders,
        her skinny legs dangling over his chest
like the straps on a life-preserver

as he positions his slipper
            onto the wire, shifts his weight
forward, onto that leg

entirely. I don't know
            why it matters to me
that matter itself endures,

dusty, or rusted, busted or
            unexpectedly whole, untouched
by time. I have long pondered this,

so suppose that I never will know,
            although I have my theories.
I suppose I will go to junk shops

until I can no longer walk, no longer
            know what lies before me,
strange as if I have never seen it before,

or, you never know, strange to me
            because it is strange, and always
was strange, treasured

for beauty, or utility, or reasons
            beyond understanding,
a monument to the great who-knows-what.

My Father's Feet

My father's feet were
the feet of a Greek statue,
long and narrow, with
a large square toe, but
tender. At the ocean
he hopped across
the sand, wincing
at broken clamshells
and brittle sea grass.
At the lake he ran
across jagged rocks
to plunge with relief
into the icy water.

Of the Aegean Sea
my father would have
said, *It's got nothing
on our Cayuga Lake.*

My father was not
a good swimmer, his kick
a booming fountain
as he labored.
He did not float,
as did my mother,
with her feathery kick
and the easy glide
he always praised
as he smiled at her
while toweling our hair.

On the day his father died, my father
sat tall in the brown armchair
and cried without covering his face,
his feet heavy on the carpet
in their thick-soled shoes.

To me he was Abraham Lincoln.

There is no record
of Lincoln's feet,
except that he walked
barefoot to school.
In the statues, he always
wears boots, plain,
without strap or buckle.

Like Lincoln, my father
cared nothing for fashion
of any type. For him,
the ancient truths:
Do unto others.
Cast not the first stone,
unless you are at a lake
and the stone is smooth
and flat and fits, just
so, in your palm.
Then, definitely cast
the first stone.
Show your children how
to cast the second stone,
the third. Then,
agree it is more fun
to collect the stones,
wash them, and carry
them home, where
they will be lost
and then forgotten.

They are just stone.

First Place

"Groomers Bring Dream Worlds to Life on Canine Canvases,"
—*New York Times*, April 19, 2010

Last year, Angela Kumpe outdid herself,
First Place, Dog Topiary,
for *Homage to Elvis*, one side

of her standard poodle sculpted into the King's face,
the dog's other side dyed and shaved into a royal blue
electric guitar, Elvis' plump hand perched lightly upon it,

each of his fingernails a pearl five-per-card shirt button,
glued as Angela listened to *Love Me Tender, Love Me
True,* a vinyl record of old Elvis singing young Elvis, over

and over, as long as it took for the glue to dry.
But this year? How does one follow a blue ribbon? This
was Angela's biggest question until February, when

her mother, Angela's muse and biggest fan, died,
this year's competition now nothing Angela could consider,
the *Times* reports, until she got the idea

to create an homage to her mother, although her mother
was not as famous as Elvis, and not especially musical.
This year's entry would be topiary of grief's lush landscape,

Angela's loyal hirsute poodle again pressed into service,
his wiry coat sculpted, along the spine, into a woman
lying with head-on-shoulder, her arms draped loosely around the dog's neck.

Having gotten a late start, Angela races against time, the *Times* reports.
She teases, dyes, tufts. She tucks the fur woman's wild orange hair
into a blue ribbon, Angela striving, she says, for *grieving Pre-Raphaelite angel,*

although the woman resembles one of those dolls
of clear pantyhose stuffed with cotton batting,
its swollen face embroidered with black thread, its mouth

an abdominal-surgery scar before healing has begun. Today,
Angela sprinkles silk leaves and plastic petals across the woman,
and the dog the woman would embrace if she could.

Tonight, for the competition, Angela Kumpe will wear a white dress
with silver wings. She will smile, position her four-legged masterpiece
against a silvery curtain, set a toy harp near

the poodle's undyed, unadorned tail.
Angela has left the dog's head and tail untouched, as if the dog
carries a sandwich board of grief, without itself being grief,

the dog merely the loyal and loving bearer of grief,
grief that will greet you at the door each time you come home,
grief that will lie beside your bed as one hot tear slides.

Angela has kept the dog, it seems, untouched by grief,
as she has kept some part of herself untouched by grief, the better
to honor her mother, to shape and frame this statement

made elsewhere in bronze, in verse, in song:
a mother's death makes the angels cry. So says Angela Kumpe
of the shears and combs and clippers, Angela of the vegetable dye

and glitter, Angela of the silk leaves and plastic petals,
Angela who knows that grief is not easy. Grief is hard work.
Grief is long work. Near hideous is grief.

Toy Harp

It was my job
to glue the pegs
to the pine frame
stained to look like oak,

then to set the harp
on a long bench
with its brethren,
to dry. No one need

turn the peg
to tighten the string
of a toy harp, tuned,
as any of us,

to one eternal pitch.
If you think my days
were long, you are right.
And you are young.

I folded my dark braid
into a blue hairnet.
At the end of that same day
my hair fell silver.

In this I was not alone,
which has been both
my joy and my sorrow.
After completion

the toy harp is not
to be touched, except
by light, by
of course dust.

I learned not to make
more of things
than they are in my hands,
which once were strong.

People like the idea
of angels and heaven. They need
something to remind them
of a world beyond

this world, where I
braided my sister's hair
and she brushed then braided mine,
we walked together to work.

I Will Wash Your Stockings

after a letter to aviatrix Katherine Stinson, circa 1916

I will wash your stockings.

Forgive me if this is something
I should not say.

It is a simple offer of one sister
to another, or of an aunt.

I am ten years older than you,
Miss Stinson, *Girl of the Skies*,

but I drive a car.
You alone know this.

I climb into my brother's Model T
on days he takes the wagon to town.

In the dust field behind the barn
I drive in circles.

It tests my nerves to tell this
to you, who lifts

your long hair into a leather cap,
drifts higher than birds

in a machine made by men.
I have read that you write in the sky

with smoke. Saturday next,
I will stand, one among hundreds,

at the fairground. I will wear a straw
hat, green ribbon at the throat,

and gloves of pale blue.
I will not speak unless you nod.

One needs clean stockings.
To wash your stockings would be my honor.

Giorgio Morandi Spent His Life

Giorgio Morandi
spent his life
painting bottles,
watercolors and
oils, in greens &
golds and blues.
Thick-walled
bottles, hand-blown or
mass-produced, it did
not matter to him. He'd
paint one bottle repeatedly,
for years, specifically, one
edge of the bottle, lip to base,
where light touched it. He
painted the light by leaving
the paper bare, a white sliver,
to mirror the shape of the
bottle's other edge, lost in
darkness. This was his life's
work: a small collection of
bottles, the light source
unidentified, the small canvas
a vessel for argument as to the
capacity of one sliver of light
to balance the dark.

Turquoise Shoes

I want the turquoise shoes in the shop window
because they shine like the Mediterranean Sea,

which I have never seen except in magazines
and the window of the travel agency beside my dentist,

these shoes I guess called *mules* because walking
in them is like climbing a rocky hillside

in relentless sun, while pebbles break loose and tumble
to a gorge below. New shoes are adventure. They transform

the wearer, if only temporarily, but what is not temporary?
And what, I ask, is the price of not celebrating the temporary?

In these shoes, with their lining of cherry-pink silk
that would kiss my instep with each difficult stride, I would own

my desire, which lavishly includes the need to be free of desire,
for these turquoise shoes are the last shoes I would ever need.

In these shoes I would lie on a chaise lounge,
slowly crossing one leg over the other, letting one turquoise marvel

dangle from my toe, as does Elaine de Kooning, in the home movie
where she drags on her cigarette and laughs, her mouth open wide,

already the drink killing her, killing the man she will never stop
loving. Elaine, what makes me think I can cast off

the heavy dark shoes of the land-locked,
the shoes laced through grommets and tied securely

at the ankle? Elaine, in your round-neck sweater,
your Capri-length pants, your lipstick, your shiny hair,

Elaine reclining on the chaise lounge and laughing,
what do we need? What do we think we need?

Sally, I Need You to Stand beside Me

Yaddo, 2009
for Sally Gross

Sally, I need you to stand beside me

in the grass and show me again how

to turn my head so my chin aligns

with my right shoulder, and then how

to place my left hand, open and loose,

against my right shoulder blade, palm

outwards, knuckles light upon the wing.

You watched me watch you, follow you,

as next you raised your right arm, up, then

up, and over your head, your outstretched

hand slowly cupping the air, then cupping

the crown of your head. *Gently,* you said,

as you showed me. *Gently,*

pull your head toward your shoulder.

Nearly each morning I do this, but I know

there was more to it. I have hoped that

some morning the rest will come to me

as the words of the whole prayer will

come if the words are spoken quickly,

without thought, but then I gave up

that hope, resigned to savoring a smaller

part of what you taught. I remember

the wide lawn gold as straw, sun-burnt,

as we stood under the wide-trunked maple,

where the grass was damp and soft,

so green it was blue. Barefoot. Our

sandals soles-up in the grass.

The Sun

The sun is tired of rising early.
        It retires. It moves

to a farm. Bad choice.
        It moves to the city, a penthouse.

The sun has invested well.
        It has a private elevator and a view

of the park. Leather sofa, palms.
        The sun can do what it wants.

The sun asks itself
        —whom else would it ask?—

Where should I travel first?
        This is a hard question. The sun

has been everywhere. It says,
        One thing I know: *how to travel*

light. The sun cracks itself up,
        always has. *Sky's the limit*,

it says. The sun decides,
        OK, the rainforest, off-season.

No, Italy, whenever. The sun wants
        gelato, where gelato began.

It wants to walk fully around
        the Pietà, wants to see

not only the bright side, but the dark.
        It wants to go off-grid, incognito,

rogue, commando. It wants to be
        a free agent. It wants to sit

in the shade, to nap
        in the afternoon.

It wants one of those linen caps,
        flat and visored. It wants to tilt

the cap, just so, and forget
        it's up there.

Woodpecker

Known for your blunt beak beating against bark,
your voice described *impatient, loud,* and *slurred,*
you are not Peterson's favorite bird.
Your grating sound is nothing like the lark.
It's more like the tire-chain's shudder, torque,
as the snowplow fights downshift into third.
Tree-clung, chisel-billed, wood-boring bombard,
you are not spring except the grinding work

of spring: clearing fallen branches, raking
dead leaves, piling stone onto stones. Thick beak
hacking bark is your truest song, clacking
knock-knock-knock, loud, unapologetic.
Unlike the birds that trill and soar, you moor.
You drill, pursuing spring's interior.

Famously Inhospitable

Famously inhospitable, Cézanne
stands in the front doorway

of his white house,
one hand on his cane,

the other hand holding a chair
that appears in many of his paintings.

It is a plain wooden chair,
as can be found

in any country kitchen.
From under his hat brim,

Cézanne stares into the camera
such that one feels

he will not offer the photographer a seat.
He will not carry out a table

and a bottle of wine,
and wake tomorrow with a headache.

Cézanne will set down the chair
and pull the door tight behind him.

He will say, *Good day.*
Meaning the light. Meaning *Goodbye.*

Edward Hopper's Paint Box

When you see Edward Hopper's paint box
      your first thought is *tetanus*, the rusted razor blades
for sharpening pencils, the painting knives
      like tiny sand-blasted pie-servers, for applying paint
impasto, for working oils while wet.
      You might stare happily at the scraps of sandpaper,
at the brittle-bristled brushes still flecked
      with gray-shot yellows, with greens infused with blue,
but who, you think, would willingly take into her hand
      even the pencil, even the small cotton rag,
and risk what they exact?

Secret of Happiness

after "Two Unfinished Cézannes Discovered at the Barnes,"
—*New York Times,* February 21, 2015

Perhaps this is the secret of happiness: selecting, from all of our questions,
one, and pursuing the answer without question, as does Denis Coutagne,

president of the Paul Cézanne Society, who spends his days walking
the stony, serrated grasses of Mont Sainte-Victoire, to find where

Cézanne stood when he sketched this unfinished view
of the Massif de l'Etoile, discovered on the back of a watercolor

removed from its frame for cleaning: a limestone peak,
in the foreground a manor house and a farmhouse no longer standing.

Denis Coutagne is apparently happy at the end of another long day,
betrays to the journalist no sign of fatigue or muscle strain,

although it cannot be easy to have climbed a mountain today, and
it cannot be easier to know you must climb it again tomorrow,

and climb it while carrying a replica of Cézanne's stool,
with its thick wooden legs, its tiny leather seat

on which the artist arranged his ample posterior.
Cézanne was not a small man except in the hills, although

from a distance his blue jacket could seem a lake or a field
of lavender, as Denis Coutagne is not a large man except in the field

of art historians, who seldom walk through any grass at all,
nor mop their foreheads as they pant on the side of a mountain.

Denis Coutagne betrays no discomfort with being addressed
by his first name, bold American habit, perhaps due to his years

of straining to see through someone else's eyes.
Some might call this the secret of happiness:

stepping out of oneself and into another,
which is like being on holiday with one light bag.

This is the lone concern of Denis Coutagne: where
did the great artist pause, set down his pack,

and settle his three-legged stool?
Where, not why.

Truthfully

I've been told that when someone says *truthfully* you should disbelieve
everything this person has said, but, although this may be good advice,
I truthfully can say my most prized possession is a purple cotton dress

printed all over with tiny white splotches that read as flowers or puddles,
where wax applied to the fabric resisted the dye, the dress
worn thin as a handkerchief in the twenty-five years since I bought it

at a flea market in New York City, from a dancer selling her clothes
to follow a troupe to Europe, where I thought I would never travel.
I wore the dress in France and in England, where I stood at the train station

at Coventry, thinking perhaps I was pregnant, and would raise our child alone,
thinking that he would fly across the ocean to me, crying the tears he had shed
as he drove me to the train in his little blue car with the steering wheel

on the wrong side. I wore, over the purple dress, a navy blue suit jacket
from the 1940s, its matching skirt long lost. And, truthfully, I looked great,
like a young Greer Garson, although did she ever look young?

Wasn't she always the serious girl with the amused eyes?
But isn't it seriousness that betrays our youth? Geoffrey—
I will call him Geoffrey—Geoffrey and I had been serious, meaning

intent upon making our lives one life. In my purple dress I stood
at the edge of the train platform, looking down at the wooden rail-ties.
Tiny star-shaped flowers grew between the ties, and swayed

on their long stems, in the breeze over the steel rails. It was hard to
believe how little soil it takes for some seeds to hold, root.
The flowers were cadmium yellow, each with a pale greenish-blue center,

and nothing has ever been more vivid to me, neither before nor since,
truthfully. I use the word for what it is: a pause where desire for truth
resides, and fear of truth. Hundreds of yellow flowers, identical, nearly.

Song After Years for the Couple
Who Owned the Country Pub

The Midlands was cool that August
only after sunset, which came slowly, and late,
from a sky that stayed blue all night,
and there was a couple,

middle-aged, who owned a pub
guarded by a peacock kept in a wooden pen.
Its cry was that of an infant, but so loud
at its call the stars themselves would scatter.

Small round tables had been carried outdoors,
some as far as the adjoining field, and so moonlight
touched the lip of our wine bottle, and my love's
blond beard, coarse against my fingertips,

our brief tenderness begun.
The man and woman who owned the pub
stood either side of a far table, placed their hands upon it.
They looked into each other's eyes, and they lifted

the table from the grass,
carried it toward the pub, and in.
Table after table they carried, slowly, haltingly,
for each table was heavier than the last

and so asked more of the couple,
both each and together,
each table a bright disk of moonlight, floating
and settling, and floating again.

20th Century Suitcase

From years behind winter coats in the attic, it rises.

It sways from upstairs to down, porch to yard

to base of the maple tree, where it circles

to rest beside a knuckled root, a hand-lettered sign,

20th Century Suitcase $5, its pocked lock locked,

a suitcase so light it might contain nothing

but the smell of dust, of cigarette, of mothball, of cedar,

starch, scorched cotton, of blood, ink, urine, wine, dark medicine

spilled from a dark bottle. From the street, this suitcase

looks like leather, instead of cardboard thickened with layers

of newspaper—headlines, box scores, want ads—

and stiffened with a thick coat of brown paint,

this suitcase homemade, made from need,

and from a need to make with one's own hands,

for one or two hours, a world

where there is no war map nailed to a wall,

there is no shawl knotted over a knot of clothes

to serve as suitcase such as this one, which is so light

perhaps it contains a blue nightgown too fine to wear,

or a ribbon-tied stack of thin letters. A brass key dangles.

A brass key dangles from its handle, from a flat string

like the lace, dear God, on a doll's calf-leather shoe,

  dear God who dares us to pay our $5

for the 20th century suitcase, to carry it home,

  this bright Saturday early in the 21st century. All afternoon

God watches as each of us walks across the suburban lawn,

  kneels before the suitcase. He watches as we rise

with it, we carry it in a small circle, deciding: it is too heavy

  for us to carry, whatever reason we have given

to our reason for traveling light.

Nest

One morning there it is,
        inside the left front corner
                of the porch roof,
jammed into the gap,

a fist-sized tangle of grass
        out of nowhere,
                as if a crow flew it
in, ready-made,

which seems no more unlikely
        than the slow accumulation
                of grass blades, twigs,
the red cellophane strip

from a cigarette packet
        thrown into the hedges.
                There is no telling how long
the nest hung there

while I walked past
        carrying groceries,
                thumbing keys.
One morning I look up,

and there it is.

I have never told David
        that for the first two years of
                our marriage, I fell asleep
remembering, room by room,

the apartment where I had lived
        alone: the living room's
                sky blue cast-iron radiator,
the deep kitchen sink with two faucets.

Before I could sleep,
      I needed to feel at home,
            which eventually happened
without my noticing.

The bird's nest
      seems barely one object,
            barely an aggregate:
grasses crushed together, not woven.

The nest is, at best, a tangle,
      which is what we were told
            was happening
inside of my mother,

tangles inside of her brain,
      so that she would ask me
            if I wanted more tea, and
then ask me if I wanted more tea, and

then again she would ask,
      so that I learned
            never to set the cup down.
I would hold it

with both hands,
      lift it repeatedly
            to my lips, drinking
the emptiness.

David and I think that the birds—
      we think sparrows—
            lived in the nest,
three days at most.

We heard tiny cheeps. Once we saw
        wings flutter,
                then spiral up,
over the roof.

We agreed to leave the nest
        there, leave it be,
                although neither of us
can say when we agreed.

Theremin

It is said that most people, given the choice,
        would rather read about God than meet God,
as most people probably would prefer

reading about the theremin, first electronic instrument,
        rather than hearing it: metal pipe sunk into a chunk
of wood riddled with wire, played by waving one's hands

in the air surrounding the pipe, stroking and cupping
        what seems simply air but is chock full
of more than we know, even these 100 years after

Leon Theremin tinkered in his basement, believing
        in this instrument that horror movies
would come to employ for any scene requiring eerie-

ness, its one note stretched like a squirrel
        in a metallic stocking. Leon Theremin,
with slicked-back hair and tortoise-shell eyeglasses,

buttoned black topcoat, like God, possessed a reserve
        not conducive to conversation. Leon hunkered
to his work, in his idea of Heaven: one light bulb,

wood-handled tools and small drawers,
        a long bench upon which he could
nap, for he rose early, knowing some things

appear once and never again.
        Leon believed in a song
that is beyond the human body,

beyond one's hands or one's mouth,
        a song made entirely
of the world's poor materials

somehow charged, somehow raising
        one's hands to cup and scoop
one moment seamlessly to the next:

music which lifts one's arms shoulder-high
        as if to dance with an invisible partner
one takes on faith

also hears this mysterious elastic song,
        though it be a stretch to call this
song, this singular note

that holds all one dares to pour into it—
        as Leon Theremin pours himself
into creating this instrument that no one loves

except in moments brief
        as we understand ourselves to be
brief, and stretched to sing of this.

Crude Angel

My angel is the crude angel at the door
of Our Lady of Perpetual Light,
the angel who waits outside the church,

at the top of three flights of black marble.
Its thick wings appear to sprout
from a granite tarp,

as if the sculptor abandoned
the angel's body, the bowed head
with featureless face,

so as to fathom the angel's hands:
folded in prayer, a prayer-fist
like a flame arisen from stone

as the Savior is said to have risen.
My angel's blocky wrists rest
upon a gown with folds so broad,

so flat, it is hard to tell if my angel
kneels or sits, or if, beneath the gown,
my angel stands,

its body broken in some way
that the faithful understand
themselves to be broken.

My angel drags itself to the door
of this church it will never enter.
Nor will my angel rise into the air,

my angel exhausted by the weight
of the stone of which it is made,
as we are exhausted by the stone

of which we are made,
we who love the angel's heavy,
useless wings, wings

that make us imagine
rising, on nothing
one can see with the eyes.

Spearmint

You know when you can't believe
        that you believe?
When   flash

there is light,
        and you have seen—
not *see*, which is a slow filling,

but *have seen*, which is sudden,
        and full of the emptiness
of what is now gone—

you have seen
        the far side of light?
For me, it was spearmint,

one leaf placed on my palm
        by the friend of a friend of
an acquaintance, one of six

or seven of us, likely none
        of whom remembers, these
years later,

one spring morning
        we hiked a hillside
so steep our fingertips touched

the damp grass,
        where we, along the way,
stopped, stood, to breathe

more deeply in. He,
        whoever he was, plucked
one leaf, and one more,

which he handed
        to me, and I did
what he did:

I tore it in two,
        placed one half
atop my bottom teeth, and

bit,
        the taste of mint
electric, my body,

inside, bright as a firefly, there,
        inside the morning's pearly fog.
You must trust me. I, too,

dislike it: received idea
        instead of idea received, gift,
the surprise that one can be

given belief, can be given faith,
        of any kind, as simply
as that, without words.

Dubbing Room

Sony Pictures Studio, Culver City, CA

We crowd into the small booth, stare out
        at the man kissing his arm, his mouth pressing
the back of his hand so his loose fist bobs

like the head of a baby, nursing, sucking
        with furious instinct, its whole body gulping
with pleasure, unlike this professional

whose pleasure we imagine the measured sigh
        of a job well done, this pucker and soft pull,
this wetting the lips precisely, so they will not chap

as he works, his one eye on the screen.
        Two actors clothed only in pink light
lie on a beach, their kisses falling short

of even the latest sound equipment, and so
        their kisses are supplied today, as we watch.
The tall, heavyset man wears a plaid shirt,

one sleeve rolled to the elbow.
        The kiss begins, it seems, not in his lips,
but in his hand, lips responding to the rise

and fall of his right hand, which he supports
        with his left, for control, or maybe for comfort,
to ease the ache in his right shoulder and the crook

of his neck, although he may court pain
        to inform these kisses, for the actors seem full
of sorrowful ardor—there, in the Pacific's rising tide.

He turns his hand over, now kissing the underside
        of his forearm, where the skin is petal-smooth.
I cannot turn away from him, despite the beautiful

lovers, twice life-size on the movie screen,
        embracing in the lapping water.
I stare at the man at the microphone,

who leans forward with something like tenderness,
        but both more and less than tenderness:
memory's enactment of love's keen attention.

He breathes deeply, slowly, makes small sounds
        in a language entirely spit and flesh.
In the soundproof booth, where we can say

anything, we stare and say nothing.
        If something is not real, does one feel
more intensely? Why can we say nothing,

not even to ourselves, as we watch
        what seems, although it is not,
what it would be to each love ourselves

and to stand thus before strangers,
        to roll up our sleeves
and, without fanfare or shame, get on with it?

Suzanne Cleary was born and raised in Binghamton, New York, but has lived in the metropolitan New York City area for over 30 years. Her full-length poetry collections are *Crude Angel* and *Beauty Mark* (BkMk Press), *Trick Pear* and *Keeping Time* (Carnegie Mellon). Her awards include a Pushcart Prize, the Cecil Hemley Memorial Award of the Poetry Society of America, and the John Ciardi Prize (for Beauty Mark). She teaches as core faculty in the low-residency MFA in Creative Writing Program of Converse College.

CRUDE ANGEL

ALSO BY SUZANNE CLEARY

Trick Pear
Keeping Time
Beauty Mark